F. (Frank) Brinkley, Arthur J Mundy,
Kakuzo

Okakura

Japan: described and illustrated by the Japanese

F. (Frank) Brinkley, Arthur J Mundy,
Kakuzo

-

Okakura

Japan: described and illustrated by the Japanese

ISBN/EAN: 9783741122637

Manufactured in Europe, USA, Canada, Australia, Japa

Cover: Foto ©Thomas Meinert / pixelio.de

Manufactured and distributed by brebook publishing software
(www.brebook.com)

F. (Frank) Brinkley, Arthur J Mundy,
Kakuzo

Okakura

Japan: described and illustrated by the Japanese

F. (Frank) Brinkley, Arthur J Mundy,
Kakuzo

Okakura

Japan: described and illustrated by the Japanese

SECTION
VI

JAPAN

IX.

RELIGION AND RITES.

ESTERN students of Buddhism are wont to say that the religion has for its basis the unreality of everything, and for its goal non-existence; that it regards man's life on earth as a link in a continuous chain of probations, to the length of which every sin adds something, so that salvation may not be reached until three immeasurable æons have lapsed.

Such is not the Buddhism of Japan. The creed, as first preached to the Japanese, was very simple. It prescribed five negative precepts and ten positive virtues, of which it is enough to say that were they practised to the letter, a high standard of morality would have been reached. The five negative precepts were, not to kill, not to be guilty of dishonesty, not to be lewd, not to speak untruths, not to drink intoxicants; the ten virtues were, to be kind to all sentient beings, to be liberal, to be chaste, to speak the truth, to employ gentle and peacemaking language, to use refined words, to express everything in a plain, unexaggerated manner, to devote the mind to moral thoughts, to practise charity and patience, and to cultivate pure intentions. These injunctions the disciple was asked to accept with unreasoning assurance. *Shinto*, as we have seen, furnished no code nor formulated any commandment. Buddhism pursued precisely the opposite plan. It issued a guiding canon of the utmost precision. But it refrained from any exposition of motives. Its method tallied exactly with that prescribed by teachers of the ideographic script which had then become the vehicle for transmitting all learning to Japan. Just as the student of the foreign symbols began by mastering their sounds and shapes and was afterwards inducted into their meanings, so an inquirer at the portals of Buddhism was first shown the letter of the law, and when he had learned how to obey, received an explanation of the principles underlying it. In the opening stage of discipline, his own salvation constituted his sole motive of conduct; in the subsequent stage of enlightenment, he developed an ardent desire to save others also. But in both alike, salvation was separated from him by an interval which his individual exertions could not bridge. Is it not easy to conceive that the great majority of the new creed's disciples never passed beyond the first stage: and is it not easy also to see that to the plebeian and proletariat classes, banished beyond the range of *Shinto* instincts and the pale of its privileges, this arithmetically precise and comfortably explicit doctrine of the Buddha offered a welcome moral refuge?

But the difference between the ardent practicality of the Japanese mind and the dreamy patience of Oriental dispositions in general, quickly affected the reception accorded to the new creed. In its moral precepts there was nothing that could be called a revelation to the members of the patrician caste, nor did its immeasurably deferred hope constitute any attraction compared with their own prospect of certain admission after death to the ranks of the deities. Even the plebeian wanted something more tangible than a heaven from which he was separated by an eternity of effort. Thus Buddhism received its first Japanese modification. A sect[1] arose, preaching that beatitude meant knowledge of the "Lotus Law;" that the attainment of that knowledge insured immediate entry into Buddhahood, and that the ancient deities whom Japan worshipped were but manifestations of the Buddha. Such adaptations quickly won for Buddhism a strong title to popular regard. It ceased to be an alien creed and became a liberal expansion of the indigenous faith.[2] It secured to the patrician his old privileges while extending them to the plebeian.

But there remained in this new conception two deterrent elements. To reach the knowledge which opened the gate to salvation it was essential that the disciple should free himself from worldly concerns and influences; should stand aloof from workaday existence; should banish all sense of the beautiful and should become absorbed in meditating on absolute truth.[3] Such a programme repelled the average Japanese. He found it admirable to worship the Buddha of "infinite light and life," and comfortable to think that the state of blessedness might be attained by the work of a single life-span. He readily adjusted his feet to the first three steps of progress,— obedience to the precepts of morality, regulation of food and clothing and the choice of a suitable house,— but when he came to the fourth, when he had to accept the necessity of turning his back on the busy world and harmonizing his faculties for a meditative career, the demand overtaxed his docility. Besides, the "Lotus Law" dealt in mysteries beyond comprehension. Its teachings lapsed into a vagueness, its doctrines extended to a comprehensiveness, that bewildered common intelligence. Soon a new system was elaborated. The omnipresent spirit of truth became the centre of the "diamond world" of noumena and the source of organic life in the world of phenomena. To reach to the realization of the truth two ladders were revealed, an intellectual and a moral, two canons, each of ten precepts, easy to comprehend and not deterrently difficult to practise. At the head of all virtues stood a charity to which the Christian apostle's celebrated definition might aptly have been applied. The scope of this pre-eminent virtue was described with minutely practical accuracy. It included the digging of wells, the building of bridges, the making of roads, the maintenance of one's parents, the support of the church, the nursing of the sick, the

---

[1] The Tendai (heavenly command) sect, founded by Dengyo Daishi in 805 A. D., under Imperial auspices. It had its chief headquarters at the celebrated monastery of Hiyei-zan.

[2] It was from this time that Shinto and Buddhism became commingled into the form of creed known as Ryobu-Shinto.

[3] Fate, with its proverbial irony, decreed that the monastery where this unworldly and meditative sect had its headquarters should have a history resonant with the clash of arms. The monks of Hiyei-zan became, from an early date, a community of soldiers.

succoring of the poor and the duty of recommending these same acts to others. There were further noble precepts and there was also an elaborate system of daily worship and prayer. All idea of abstention from the affairs of every-day life disappeared, and the hereafter became, not a state of absolute non-existence (*nirvana*), but the "infinite perception of a beatific vision;" a condition in which each of the saved formed one of a band of " great intercessors, pleading continually for their ignorant and struggling brethren upon earth that they might ' attain to the same heights of perfect enlightenment and bliss.' "[1]

This is the *Shingon* sect. the sect of the "True Word," the sect of the *Logos*, founded in 816 A. D. by one of the greatest of Japanese religious teachers, Kobo Daishi. So far as it has been here set down, its outlines might easily be adapted to a partial picture of Christianity. There is a great presiding spirit; there is an ethical system that the followers of the Nazarene might indorse; there is a band of interceding saints in heaven; there is an eternity of happiness; there is an everlasting law of retribution, every infraction of the moral code entailing a commensurate penalty; there are incarnations of the Supreme Being— not one incarnation, indeed, but several— whose mission is to lead men to the knowledge of the

A LOTUS GARDEN.

truth. But if such affinities with Christianity exist, so also do differences. There is a belief in previous existences and in their unknown sins, by which the devotee is kept entangled in the cycle of life and death; there is prayer to the gods of the country, the *Shinto* deities; and there is worship of ancestors, in a modified form, indeed, but still worship.

With this development of Buddhism the Japanese may be said to have remained content for three hundred and sixty years. Then, in the presence of perpetual wars, spoliations and miseries, the creed took another shape, a shape that reflected the conditions of the time. Salvation by faith was preached. The world had fallen upon such evil days that a cry of despair went up to Amida, the Buddha of endless life and light. Men were taught that works could not avail, and that in blind trust, aided by the repetition of ceaseless

[1] Lloyd's " Developments of Japanese Buddhism," a work of high value to students of this subject.

formulæ, lay the only hope of salvation. Such was the doctrine of the sect of the Pure Land (*Jodo*), founded by Honen Shonin (1174 A. D.). It attracted numerous disciples. The comforting tenet, that by simple trust in Amida during life, admittance to his paradise might be secured after death, perfectly suited the dejected mood of the age, and would, indeed, suit the mood of men in all ages antecedent to the millennium.[1]

Fifty years later another sect was born, a child of the "Pure Land," namely, the Spirit sect.[2] The latter did not supplant the former, but rather supplemented it. In this new system love was added to trust. Grateful remembrance of the mercies of Amida and faith in his willingness and power to save, now sufficed to secure salvation and to keep the devotee's feet in the true path. There were other differences also. The disciple learned, not that Amida waited until the hour of a man's death to conduct him to paradise, but that the coming of the saviour was present and immediate; that he took up his abode at once, even during life, in the heart of the saved. The doctrine essential to all forms of Buddhism remained,—the doctrine that misfortune in this world had its root in some evil wrought in a previous state of existence,—but it received the adjunct that neither Amida nor any other Buddha might be invoked to interrupt the natural sequence of cause and effect, and, as a logical corollary, amulets, spells and all such aids were interdicted. The devotee was no longer invited to become a priest, to abandon his home and embrace celibacy. All in every rank and of every calling were entitled to entertain an equal hope of salvation. The priests themselves ceased to observe some of the vetoes that chiefly distinguished them from laymen. They married, ate meat, and, if desirable, replaced the stole by the surcoat. They learned in the domestic circle those sympathies and appreciations that a celibate can never develop. This "Spirit sect" is the largest in Japan. With its parent, the "Pure Land sect," it possesses more than one third of all the temples in the country. It is full of vitality. Its doctrines as to the origin of the world, the sphere of providential functions, original sin, the efficacy of prayer, the immortality of the soul and the resurrection of the body, do not so greatly shock ordinary intelligence, or make such large demands on unreasoning credulity, as do the corresponding tenets preached from Western pulpits.

We now come to the last sect that need be noticed here—a sect that has attracted considerable observation among Occidental students of Japanese Buddhism. It is the sect of the "Flower of the Law" (*Hokke-shu*), founded (1253 A. D.) by Nichiren (the Lotus of Light), one of the noblest and most picturesque figures among Japanese "saints." The essential difference between the creed of Nichiren and the creeds of all his predecessors is that he preached a god, the prime and only great cause. They showed to their disciples a chain of cause and effect, but had nothing to say about its origin; he taught that the first

---

[1] This sect received much patronage from the Imperial Court, as well as from the Tokugawa Shoguns. The great temple, Zojo-ji, which stands among the Tokugawa mausolea in Shiba, belongs to the *Jodo-shu* (*shu* = sect).

[2] *Shin-shu*, called also *Monto-shu* (sect of gate disciples), and *Ikko-shu* (undivided sect), founded by Shinran in 1224 A. D.

link in the chain was the Buddha of original enlightenment, of whom all subsequent Buddhas, Sakyamuni and the rest, were only transient reflections. Nichiren thus reached the Christian conception of a god in whom everything lives, moves and has its being; an omnipotent, omnipresent and omniscient deity. All phenomena, mental and material, in all time and space, were declared by him to have only subjective existence in the consciousness of the individual. The differences and distinctions observed by the ordinary man were imaginary and misleading; had no foundation in fact. In the eyes of the Buddha there was identity where the vulgar saw variety. To know the underlying sameness of all things, to understand the oneness of the perceiver and the perceived, — that was true wisdom. It followed that this world, so full of evils to mortal vision, did not differ from paradise in the Buddha's sight. To the enlightened, all worlds were equally beautiful. "Hence, to proclaim the identity of this evil or phenomenal world with the glorious underlying reality, or noumenon; to point out the way to Buddhahood; to open the path of salvation; above all, to convince the people that one and all of them might become Buddhas, here and now, — that was the mission of the sect of Nichiren." [1]

Thus the colors that Buddhism took in its transmission through the Japanese mind were all bright hues. Death ceased to be a passage to mere non-existence and became the entrance to actual beatitude. The ascetic selfishness of the contemplative disciple was exchanged for a career of active charity. The endless chain of cause and effect was shortened to a single link. The conception of one supreme all-merciful being, forced itself into prominence. The gulf of social and political distinctions that yawned so widely between the patrician and the plebeian, separating them by a chasm which seemed well-nigh impassable, and all the

OX CART.

Much of the heavy teaming is done by man power, but oxen and horses are occasionally used. Notice the straw sandals with which the oxen are shod to protect their hoofs.

other unsightlinesses of the world, became subjective *eidola* destined to disappear at the first touch of moral light. The Buddha and the people were identified.

Turning now to the daily life of the individual we find that it was never overshadowed

[1] "The Doctrines of Nichiren;" compiled by the Right Virtuous Abbot Kobayashi; translated by Messrs. K. Tatsumi and F. H. Balfour.

by his religion. Confession of sins, repentance in sackcloth and ashes, solemn and protracted acts of worship, the terrors of an eternity of torture, — these things entered scarcely at all into the layman's existence. The temple presented itself to him as a place where the mortuary tablets of his ancestors were guarded; a place to be visited for the burning of incense at tombs and their adornment with flowers on anniversaries of the deaths of near relatives; a place for the occasional deposit of small coins in an alms chest; a place for offering up brief prayer when every-day affairs seemed in need of the Buddha's divine influence; a place where the ashes of the worshipper himself would in the end be laid to rest, and whither his own friends and relatives would come to honor his memory when he too should have received from the priests one of those beautiful and benevolent posthumous titles which they knew so well how to choose. It was all essentially practical and easy-going. If a man needed moral guidance, he went to the temple and listened to a sermon. On set days, sometimes every day, one of the priests preached. He sat before a small lectern on a dais raised a little above the wide area of the matted nave and talked to the people sitting around him on the floor. His sermon was generally of the simplest. It dealt with the affairs of common life; with the small cares of *Osandou*, the maid of all work; with the troubles of *Detchi*, the shop boy; with the woes of *O-yuki*, the danseuse, and with the perplexities of *Tarobei*, the rustic. Great ceremonies of worship might also be attended, but with these the ordinary individual had no intellectual sympathy. They were to him merely spectacular effects, solemn, splendid and impressive, but incomprehensible. If the devout watched them with awed mien, the little belles of the parish were guilty of no irreverence when they pattered up the steps leading to the lofty hall of worship, peeped in smilingly at the tonsured chanters of litanies and reciters of *sutras*, and pattered away again with just such faces of sunny unconcern as they might have worn on their way home from a dancing lesson. Buddhism, Japanese Buddhism, can never produce a Puritan or a Covenanter. It weaves no threads of solemnity or sanctimoniousness into the pattern of every-day life. Its worlds of hungry demons and infernal beings are too unsubstantial, too remote, to throw any lurid glare over the present. The festival, indeed, may be called the popular form of worship in Japan, such a festival as can be seen in October at the Ikegami temple near Tokyo on the anniversary of Nichiren, whose doctrine of the Flower of the Law has been outlined above. It is a species of gala for the huge multitude numbering some two hundred thousand — that throngs thither during the two days of the *fête*. If the tiny band of devout folks that listen to the sermon be compared with the gay crowds that roam about the beautiful woods, enjoy the enchanting landscapes and seascapes presenting themselves on every side, and frequent the various entertainments provided for their diversion by itinerant showmen, the ratio of holiness to holiday becomes very suggestive. It may be difficult for the reader to imagine the precincts of a Christian cathedral on a saint's day occupied by acrobats, jugglers, travelling menageries, performing dogs and such frivolities, while the business of prayer and preaching proceeds vigorously within the walls of the building. Yet such a conception is only partial ; it must be supplemented by another strange feature, namely, that the temple building stands open throughout the whole of one side, so that the people who happen to be praying within are virtually a part of the audience enjoying the penny shows without. Here, as everywhere in Japan, the practical sincerity of the national character shows itself. Even at a religious festival no effort to dissimulate the traits of which humanity can never divest itself is encouraged or expected. The great majority of the people come for the sake of the outing as much as to pay respect to the memory of the saint. Let them, then, enjoy themselves. Religion does not prescribe austerity of manners or asceticism of life. The Buddhas are not shocked because a monkey turns summersaults under the eaves of their sanctuaries, or a rope-dancer balances in the shadow of their shrines. In this very rope-dancer, too, the observer may see another instance of the spirit of sincerity that presides at the festival. In Europe a female gymnast dresses in flesh-colored tights and seeks to place her womanhood in suggestive evidence. The Japanese girl at the Ikegami *fête* has no such fancy. Her business is rope-dancing, not meretricious posing. The latter may be very well in its way, but has nothing to do with poising one's body on some strands of plaited hemp. Therefore the Ikegami girl who undertakes to exhibit skill in the science of equilibrium wears garments which, while they are excellently suited to the purposes of her performance, are even better qualified to divert attention from the sex of the performer. There, too, in another part of the spacious grounds, a party of priests may be seen watching the manœuvres of some highly trained birds. Why not? They are jaunty, saucy little chaffinches as ever exhibited themselves in public; and to see them skip out of their cages, bow to their trainer and to the audience, ring bells, count coins, pound rice and do the woodpecker business against every convenient post, is to conceive a new respect for bird intelligence. So the praying goes on, and the rattling of *cash* against the bars of the money chest, and the burning of incense, and the chattering of monkeys, and the shouting of showmen, and the perpetual rippling of laughter, and the babble of cheery

CREEK-SIDE, YOKOHAMA.

talk as the great good-humored multitude flows to and fro, not a bit nearer to hell or farther from heaven because its units have studied no hypocritical mien of sanctimoniousness, or been trained to deceive their deity by putting a veneer of puritanism over the instincts which he has implanted in their breasts.

But in such a crowd what proportion does the literate element bear to the illiterate, the patrician to the plebeian? And if the philosopher is there as well as the bumpkin, the savant as well as the servant, how much of pastime is the motive of each and how much of worship? That is a great question. It amounts to asking what has been the influence of Buddhism upon the educated classes in Japan. Undoubtedly that influence was once very powerful. Undoubtedly the religion possessed, at the time of its advent, numerous features strongly attractive. It brought in its company a noble literature; a literature pregnant with philosophic thought presented to the mind in attractive guise; a literature embodying every-thing that was profound and beautiful in Oriental speculation. It built for itself temples the grandeur of whose architectural proportions and the gorgeousness of whose decoration surpassed Japanese conception. Its priests manifested a spirit of activity, benevolence and self-denial that could not but impress a nation entirely strange to the spectacle of religious zeal. It found a people devoting themselves to the study of Chinese literature with all the fervor that marks their descendants' excursions into the domain of Western learning, and it presented to them a library of books within whose ideographic pages was enshrined a mine of speculative thought, a mass of obscure, intricate, subtle metaphysical suggestions that derived a semblance of profundity from their very strangeness, of magnificence from the ignorance of their students. The minute mechanism of the new system constituted an addi-tional attraction. It carried men from the simplest and vaguest of creeds to the most complex and definite; from a faith without ethical code or canons of dogma to a faith extra-ordinarily rich in both. If there is, as we know there is, a tendency in the human mind to pass from one extreme to another, it is easy to understand how gladly the feet of many turned from wandering in the trackless deserts of *Shinto* to march in the beaten paths and along the carefully graded highways of Buddhism. Further, the monasteries were the chief seats of learning. Proficiency in Buddhism was synonymous with proficiency in the Chinese language, with possession of the key to all the stores of the Middle Kingdom's learning. Yet, when we come to ask whether from this array of secular and religious arguments the conclusion may be derived that the supernatural phases of Buddhism impressed themselves upon the hearts of the educated classes, the answer must be negative. It is hard, indeed, to imagine a total lack of that kind of faith among men who, in mediæval times, contributed vast sums to support or endow temples, made them the depositories of their ancestral tablets, and repaired thither at set seasons to hear orisons chanted, *sutras* read, and sermons preached. But still more difficult is it to conceive that, had the transcendental doctrines of Buddhism sunk deep into the national mind, some evidence of the fact would not have been furnished in the growth of a philosophical literature, the product of lay pens. There is practically no such literature. On the contrary, there are plain indications that the supernatural beliefs of Buddhist teachers gradually became the object of open or covert ridicule among the learned, and were ultimately relegated to much the same place in the minds of educated men as ghost stories occupy in European or American thought to-day. In short, religion as distinguished from morality, came to be quietly ignored. Nothing survived beyond an instinctive belief in the immortality of the soul and a traditional faith in a future world peopled by the shades of parents and relatives loved in life and reverenced after death. Much of the vogue so speedily attained and so steadily retained by Confucianism is doubtless due to the subordinate place assigned to supernatural religion in that system. Confucianism, too, owing to the note of feudalism that sounds through its philosophy, has been

found to be more or less out of harmony with the spirit of Occidental civilization, and is destined, in its turn, to pass into the oblivion where so many Oriental systems lie buried. But through fourteen centuries it worked steadily and powerfully to turn the mind of educated Japan from transcendental subtleties and religious mysticism to a conviction that the only true and rational creed is one which subjects the human faculties to no excessive strain, nor asks men to accept, on the alleged authority of supernatural revelation, propositions lying wholly beyond the range of mortal intelligence. Buddhism, in the bright and comfortable garments with which Japanese genius clothed it, is the faith of the masses, but the scholar proposes to himself a simpler creed, an essentially workaday system of ethics. To be moral, honest and upright; to be guided by reason and not by passion; to be faithful to friends and benefactors; to abstain from meanness and selfishness in

SEA CAVE AT ENOSHIMA.

all forms; to be prepared to sacrifice everything to country and king,— that is the ideal of the cultured mind, and in the pursuit of it no priestly guidance is considered necessary. If a Japanese be asked to define the much-talked-of *Yamato damashii*, the spirit of Yamato,— he will do so in the words set down here.

As to the masses, the farmer, the artisan, the shopkeeper and the proletariat, when we say that Buddhism is their creed, the reader will be prepared to hear, from what has been written above, that at sacred service as well as at festival time they do not take their faith very seriously. A visitor to the temple on the day of the *sekkyo*, the day of the sermon, which has been duly advertised on a species of signboard at the entrance of the enclosure, cannot fail to note that nine tenths of the congregation are white-haired, the remainder consisting of children with a sparse admixture of adults. *Tarobei* may be there, driven by the dread that some unsettled account stands between him and the heaven which ought to have averted the typhoon from his rice-field or the insect plague from his mulberry plantation; and little *O-setsu* may be there, who, last evening, sat beside her brazier, her dimples banished and her sweet head bowed as she mused over the indissoluble chain of causation that had linked her to love troubles and a throbbing heart. But these are the exceptions. Generally the worshipper carries with him wrinkles and snowy locks, and a hope that since the affairs of the "fleeting world" have become to him as "dust before the wind," he may by pious practices acquire a vested interest in the affairs of the world to come. He can follow the sermon. It is plain, simple, adapted to the lowest order of intelligence, the even flow of its gentle precepts unimpeded by any rocks of erudition nor deepening to any profundities of transcendental philosophy. The old folks listen with comfortable reverence, and at each pause in the preacher's eloquence - eloquence sometimes of the highest order—bow their heads, roll their rosaries between their palms, devoutly murmur *Namu Amida-ton*, or whatever formula the sect prescribes, and then throw into the alms chest an offering of *cash*. The parabled mite of the widow was a farthing. The *cash* of Japan is the fortieth part of a penny, and a worshipper who launches four of these liliputian coins into the great chest has done his duty nobly. No one talks of these copper tokens as *saisen*. They are *o-saisen*. The honorific prefix belongs to them just as fully as it does to the lordly vases of silver and gold lotus that flank the altar; to the resplendent altar itself with its broad face of rosy lacquer, its richly chased and heavily gilded mountings, its furniture of fine bronze and ancient *céladon*; or to the magnificent shrine that glows with mellowed splendor in the sacred obscurity of the chancel. But beyond the sermon, beyond the throwing of *o-saisen* and the rolling of beads, what does the worshipper understand? Nothing. The *sutra* is there — the lotus law, engrossed in exquisite ideographs upon an illuminated scroll. But its texts are unintelligible. To the average Japanese they convey as little as a verse from the original Koran would convey to a cowboy. They are part of the magnificent unknown. The priest is the repository of whatever blessed knowledge they embody, the transmitter of their divine message to mankind. And the priest himself understands how to lend spectacular effect to that part of his office. When he seats himself among his congregation to preach, he wears the simplest of robes, a white or sober-hued cassock and a black stole. But when he opens the *sutra* or recites the litany, his vestments are of brocade that would serve worthily

TEA–PICKERS.

Tea is believed to have been introduced into Japan from China in 805 A. D. Though encouraged from the first by Imperial recommendations, tea-culture made little progress in Japan until the close of the twelfth century. In 1894 Japan exported fifty million pounds of tea, three fourths of which came to the United States. The home consumption is very large, as every native is a tea-drinker. The labor of picking this immense crop is performed largely by children.

to drape a throne, and might well betray the female units of his congregation into the sin of "lust of the eye" were not the precaution adopted of cutting the splendid fabric into a multitude of fragments before fashioning it into stole or cassock. Patchwork quilts are not used in Japan, and a girdle checkered with seams after the fashion of a chessboard would be a shocking solecism.

So the housewife and the belle are enabled to admire these grand brocades without coveting them.

The religious service is strikingly different from the sermon: the latter, a practical, plainly phrased adaptation of saving ethics to every-day affairs; the former, a mysterious, impressive and enigmatical display, as far

FUTU-ARA TEMPLE, NIKKO.

removed from mundane affinities as is the lotus throne itself. At one of the great temples, in a hall of worship fifty feet high, four times as many long and three times as many broad, these services may be seen by all comers. The huge hall is absolutely without decoration, except in one spot where stand the shrine and the altar, a mass of glowing gold and rich colors, mellowed by wide spaces on either side to which the daylight scarcely penetrates. Within a circular enclosure at the outer end of the nave sit a band of acolytes chanting to an accompaniment of wooden timbrels. Their voices are pitched in octaves, and the number of chanters is varied from time to time so as to break the monotony of the cadence. When this has continued for some moments, nine priests, richly robed, emerge slowly and solemnly from the back of the chancel and kneel before an equal number of lecterns ranged in line on the left of the altar. Each priest carries a chaplet of beads, and on each lectern is a missal. Then the chant of the acolytes ceases, and the priest kneeling in the middle of the line opens the *sutra* and reads aloud. One by one his companions follow his example, until the nine voices blend in a monotone, which, in turn, is varied by the same device as that previously adopted by the acolytes. After an interval, another similar band pace gravely down the chancel, and kneeling on the right of the altar, opposite the first comers, add their voices in the same cumulative fashion to the varying volume of sound. Finally, the chief priest himself emerges, attended by an acolyte, and kneels, facing the altar, at a large lectern placed between the two rows of *sutra*-readers. He confines himself at first to burning incense, and, as the fumes ascend denser and denser, the intonation of the reading priests grows more and more accelerated, until at last their words pour forth with bewildering volubility. Then suddenly this peal of resonance dies away to a scarcely audible murmur, and while its echoes are still trembling in the air they are joined by the voice of the chief priest, which by degrees absorbs them into its swelling note and then itself faints to a whisper, taken up in turn and swelled to a rolling chant by the tones of the *sutra*-readers. These alternations of intoning constitute virtually the whole ceremony. It is grave, awe-inspiring and massive in its simplicity. It captivates the senses by degrees, and lifts them at last to an ecstasy where reason ceases to discern that the components of the grand ceremony are nothing more than deftly interwoven fragments of a chanted litany, gorgeous vestments, a heart of glowing gold and soft colors in a vast sepulchre of shadow, and an edifice of noble proportions. But that analytical consciousness certainly comes to the average layman sooner or later. That he has reached it is plainly shown by his mien. The sketchy act of worship that he uses as a passport to such ceremonials bears as little proportion to their magnificence as does the fee paid at the door of a theatre to the tumultuous moods of mirth or sadness produced by the spectacle within. Nothing in which the mechanical element predominates can be permanently interesting. The Buddhist services appeal only to a narrow range of emotions and leave the intellect untouched. The adult Japanese takes little interest in them. To be a frequent temple-goer out of season, that is to say, on occasions other than those dictated by reverence to the memory of a deceased relative or friend, is to be regarded by one's neighbors as uncanny, unpractical and probably unfortunate.

The priest himself contributes nothing, either by intellectual culture or a life of conspicuous zeal and virtue, to raise his religion to a place in the people's hearts. He used to be the nation's schoolmaster as well as its scholar. The State has stepped in and relieved him of the former function; the latter title he has long lost. The example he sets is one of indolence. Now and then, in the perfunctory routine of colorless duty, he has to intone a litany that has been ringing in his ears since childhood, and always his figure looms on the horizon of the layman's life when incense has to be burned and prayer said for the soul of the departed. But for the rest he is without occupation. He is not to be found waiting with words of comfort at the bedside of the dying, or with hands of helpfulness in the hovels of the poor. Once only, at the great *Bon* festival, when the spirits of the dead revisit the homes of the living, the priest finds himself busied with ministrations. But it is an interval of only four days, and the work is lightened by its large reward, for during that brief space the major part of the year's income is collected.

The advent of Christianity has galvanized Buddhism into new life. The Western missionary came to uproot the lotus plant. His attack has resulted in making the sap circulate once more through its withered limbs. There is a sort of Buddhist revival. Schools have been established by each sect for the education of its priests; propagandists are sent out, periodicals are published. Buddhism is not dead. It is not even moribund. In the spring of 1895, the disciples of the *Monto* sect assembled in Kyoto to open a temple on the construction of which eight million *yen* had been spent, and in the transport of whose huge timbers cables made of women's hair had been used. Hundreds of thousands of believers had contributed money and material for the building; hundreds of thousands of women and girls had shorn off their tresses to weave these ropes. There is abundant life in the faith still.

This seems the proper place to say a word about the relations between Church and State in Japan. Up to the beginning of the ninth century *Shinto* had no rival in official patronage; it was virtually the sole religion of Court and country alike. A special department (*Jingi-kan*) of *Shinto* ceremonies managed all matters connected with worship and stood at the head of all public offices. From the establishment of the capital at Kyoto, however, the influence of Buddhism began to be felt, not in open opposition, but rather as an overshadowing and absorbing system which, by appropriating the chief traditional features of its rival, gradually deprived the latter of individuality and therefore of power. Still the imported faith remained long without State recognition. Its priesthood, though growing in wealth and numbers and practically autocratic within the domain of religious affairs, enjoyed no official exemptions or privileges. Their hierarchs were appointed without reference to the secular authorities and were not included in the roll of official grades. Under the Tokugawa government a change took place. Following the example of their great predecessor, Ieyasu, the *Shoguns* ruling in Edo spared no pains to cement their relations with Buddhism by extending to it ample patronage and support. Yet, even while striking monuments of that

CARPENTERS AT WORK.

munificence grew up in the splendid temples at Shiba, Uyeno and Nikko, the political status of the creed might have remained unaltered had not the advent of Christianity and the government's crusade against it led the third *Shogun*, Iyemitsu, to conceive the necessity of establishing a certain measure of State control over religious affairs. It was not an extensive control. The priesthood retained competence to elect their hierarchs, enforce their canons, and manage the details of their ecclesiastical organizations. But there was added to the body politic a new class of officials called *Jisha-bugyo*, whose duty was to administer the secular laws in all matters relating to religion and who were chosen from among the most influential nobles in the empire. The Church, in short, was removed beyond the pale of the ordinary tribunals and brought under the purview of the highest powers in the State. A hundred years later, that is to say, during the first half of the eighteenth century, there sprung up a remarkable scholastic movement which aimed at re-popularizing the ancient traditions of the indigenous faith and denouncing the tenets of Buddhism and Confucianism alike. It has yet to be determined how closely that movement was connected with the impulse which culminated in the political revolution of 1867. We may assert, at all events, that it revivified the doctrine of the divinity of the throne and that the Restoration of 1867 depended on that doctrine. Naturally, therefore, the government of the Restoration identified itself with the revival inaugurated by the great scholars Mabuchi, Motoori and Hirata a hundred years previously. The *Jisha-bugyo*, whose authority had extended to *Shinto* and Buddhism alike, were abolished and in their stead was established the *Jingi-sho*, an office which ranked above all the State departments and was practically a resuscitation of the *Jingi-kan* spoken of above. It is not to be doubted that the aim of the more radical reformers of the time was the ultimate suppression of Buddhism and the elevation of *Shinto* to the rank of the State Church. For whereas the affairs of *Shinto* received direct superintendence from the new office, those of Buddhism ceased to be recognized by officialdom; the Buddhist temples were stripped of the greater part of their large estates, and since they necessarily lost at the same time the munificent patronage that had been extended to them by the feudal nobles, a season of decadence and impoverishment overtook them. But Buddhism had twined its roots too strongly around the hearts of the people to be overthrown by an official storm. Steadily it reasserted its influence, until, in 1872, the *Jingi-sho* was replaced by the *Kyobu-sho*, an office ranking lower than its predecessor but still very high in the administrative organization. From this office the priests of the two religions received equal recognition and the same official title (*Kyodo-shoku*). Thenceforth the government's purpose of identifying the interests of Church and State gradually ceased to have practical force, until (in 1884) the ranks and titles of the priests were abolished, the various sects were declared perfectly free to choose their own superintendents and manage their own affairs, and in the administrative organization there remained only an insignificant Bureau of Shrines and Temples (*Shuji-kyoku*) to deal with questions from which the secular authority could not prudently dissociate itself. The last tie that bound the Church to the State was severed by the promulgation of the Constitution in 1889, the 27th article of which declares that, " within limits not prejudicial to peace and order and not antagonistic to their duties as subjects, Japanese subjects shall enjoy freedom of religious belief."

Shinto, however, remains the unique creed of the Imperial house. Appended to the Constitution by which freedom of conscience was so unequivocally granted to the people, were three documents, a preamble, an Imperial oath in the sanctuary of the palace, and an Imperial speech, every one of which contained words that left no doubt of the sovereign's rigid adherence to the patriarchal faith of Japan. In the preamble his Majesty said: "Having, by virtue of the glories of our ancestors, ascended the throne of a lineal succession unbroken for ages eternal; desiring to promote the welfare and to give development to the moral and intellectual faculties of our subjects who have been favored with the benevolent care and affectionate vigilance of our ancestors, and hoping to maintain the prosperity of the State in concert with our people and with their support, we hereby promulgate, etc.;" in the Imperial oath he said: "We, the successor to the prosperous throne of our predecessors, do humbly and solemnly swear to the Imperial founder of our house and to our Imperial ancestors that, in consonance with a great policy coextensive with the heavens and with the earth, we shall maintain and secure from decline the ancient form of government. . . . These laws [the Constitution] come to only an exposition of grand precepts for the conduct

STONE TORII, SUWA TEMPLE, NAGASAKI.

of the government, bequeathed by the Imperial founder of our house and by our other Imperial ancestors. That we have been so fortunate in our reign, in accordance with the tendency of the times, as to accomplish this work, we owe to the glorious spirits of the Imperial founder of our house and of our other Imperial ancestors;" and in the Imperial speech he says: "The Imperial founder of our house and our other Imperial ancestors, by the help and support of the forefathers of our subjects, laid the foundation of our empire upon a basis which is to last forever. That this brilliant achievement embellishes the annals of our country, is due to the glorious virtues of our sacred Imperial ancestors and to the loyalty and bravery of our subjects, their love of country and their public spirit." There is no ambiguity here, nor, indeed, any feebleness of language. The Mikado, looking back to the immortals as his progenitors, and persuaded that his dynasty and empire have their protection and the protection of the successive Mikados now enrolled in their ranks, believes that the past twenty-six centuries of his house's rule and his realm's integrity are an earnest of unbroken continuity awaiting both in the future. Folks in the Occident who listen with the calm born of long custom while their monarchs proclaim themselves king or emperor "by the grace of God," and who join to the echoes of their triumphal pæans a prayer for the abiding countenance of the "Lord of hosts," can scarcely claim an unqualified title to criticise the more comprehensive, though not more robust, faith of the Emperor of Japan.

The various religious ceremonials observed at Court are all on the strict lines of orthodox *Shinto*. On the first day of the first month, the *Shiho-hai* (four-quarter adoration) is celebrated. The Emperor worships the Sun Goddess, whose shrine is at Ise, as well as the Celestial and Terrestrial Deities, and makes offerings before the Imperial cenotaphs, praying for the happiness of his people and the peace of his reign. On the third of the same month, the Imperial ancestors and the deities of heaven and earth are again worshipped, and petitions, now more particularly connected with the tranquillity and prosperity of the reign, are addressed to these supernatural guardians, in a ceremonial called the *Genshi-sai* (festival of the beginning). On the eleventh of the second month the *Kigen-setsu* (memorial of the origin) is held, to commemorate the ascension of the first mortal Emperor, Jimmu. On the seventeenth of the tenth month, the first rice of the year and saké brewed from it are offered to the Sun Goddess, the ceremony being called *Kanname* (divine tasting). On the twenty-third of the eleventh month, a similar rite, the *Niiname* (new tasting) is performed, the difference being that the first fruits are now offered to all the deities. The birthday of the Emperor himself is also celebrated and four solemn mourning services are performed, one on the anniversary of the death of the late Emperor, Kōmei (30th January); the second on that of the death of the first Emperor, Jimmu (3d April); the third and fourth in memory of all the Imperial ancestors. These last two are called *Shunki-korei-sai* (worship of the Imperial spirits at the vernal equinox) and *Shuki-korei-sai* (worship of the Imperial spirits at the autumnal equinox), and take place on the spring and autumn equinoctial days, respectively.

No material differences distinguish the routine of these ceremonials: to know one is to know all. Within the palace there is a large hall, the *Kashiko-dokoro*, or place of reverence, constructed of milk-white, knotless timbers, exquisitely joined and smooth as mirrors but absolutely devoid of decoration. At one end stands a large shrine, also of snow-pure wood, with delicately chased mountings of silver gilt. It encloses models of the divine insignia and a number of long, narrow tablets of pine, on which are inscribed the posthumous titles of all the Emperors since the days of *Jimmu*. The floor is covered with rice-straw mats having borders of white damask, and within the folding doors of the shrine hangs a curtain woven out of bamboo threads. At the appointed hour, generally the gray of morning, *sakaki* boughs are laid beside the shrine and provision of incense (*shinko*) is made; after which the officials of the Bureau of Rites and those of the Imperial household file in and seat themselves on either side of the hall. The doors of the shrine are then opened, and offerings of various kinds — vegetables, fish, cloth and so forth — are carried in and ranged before it, solemn music in Japanese style being performed the while. Thereafter the princes of the blood and all officials of the two highest ranks (*shinnin* and *chokunin*), as well as the peers of the "musk chamber" (*Jako-no-ma*) and the "golden-pheasant chamber" (*Kinkei-no-ma*) enter, and when they are seated the Emperor himself appears and, proceeding slowly to the shrine, bows his head, takes a branch of *sakaki*[1] with pendent *gohei*, and having waved it in token of the purification of sins, ignites a stick of incense and places it upright in the censer, thereafter repeating a ritual (*notto*). So long as the Emperor is present in the hall all the officials remain standing. His Majesty then retires, and, on his departure, worship of the same kind but without any prayer is performed by a representative of the prince imperial, by the princes of the blood and by the various officials, each in due order of rank. Finally the offerings are removed and the shrine is closed to accompaniment of music, as before, and all retire. An interval of a few minutes succeeds, and then, once more, the officials of the household department resume their seats, preparatory to worship by the empress dowager and the empress. The routine and rites are exactly as before, but the official worshippers are different. They now include nobles of all orders, officials of the two inferior grades (*sonin* and *hannin*), *Shinto* and Buddhist superintendents and the chief priests of the *Monto* sect. The ceremony, owing to the numbers that take part in it and the unvaried solemnity of their procedure, occupies a long time, but is of the simplest character.

It is significant that the chief representatives of Buddhism join in these acts of *Shinto* worship; but since, as we have already seen, the apostles of Buddhism in Japan combined their creed with

OJI TEA HOUSE, TOKYO.

the indigenous faith by declaring, in the eighth century, that the Buddha of Light

[1] The use of *sakaki* (*cleyera Japonica*) is referred to the sylvan method of worship practised in the earliest times. A space surrounded by thick trees constituted the hall of rites. The trees were called a "sacred fence" (*himorogi*), and it seems probable that strips of the cloth offered to the deities were hung from the branches. Thus, even after a shrine had been built to receive the divine insignia (the mirror, the sword and the jewel), a bough of *sakaki* with white pendants (*gohei*) continued to be included in the paraphernalia of the ceremony of worship.

(*Dainichi Nyorai*, the Indian *Birushanabutsu*) had been incarnated as Amaterasu in Japan, as Sakya-muni in India and as Confucius in China, Buddhist hierarchs of modern times merely obey the tenets of their religion when they bow before the *Shinto* shrine in the Hall of Reverence. Christianity, however, has made no such adaptation, and it will be at once apparent that there is here a marked distinction between the attitudes of Christianity and Buddhism towards the State. It will also be apparent that to speak of a complete separation between the Church and the State is misleading. Were it the custom in England, for example, that all the officials of the central government and all the heads of religious sects throughout the realm should attend on fixed occasions in Westminster Abbey and assist at divine service according to prescribed rites, no one could think of questioning the fact that Church and State were very closely bound together. It is not to be understood that compulsion is exercised with regard to such matters in Japan. Among the body of officials who meet in the Hall of Reverence there must be many Christians. It would be possible for these men to absent themselves on the ground of sickness. In no country does the conventional element of an excuse receive more generous recognition than in Japan. The plea of "indisposition" is accepted without scrutiny and is understood to be serviceable as an explanation no less than as a reason. But if officials who profess Christianity and attend Christian places of worship made a habit of standing aloof, on whatever plea, from the services conducted by the Emperor in honor of the Sun Goddess and the spirits of the Imperial ancestors, can there be any doubt about the impression that such differentiation must ultimately produce upon the mind of the nation? In point of fact Christians do not stand aloof. They bow their heads and burn incense before the shrine in company with the disciples of Shaka and of *Shinto*. How much violence they do to their own religious convictions in thus acting, how much homage they pay to the god of expediency, it is not for us to inquire. "Men can be strangled with a strand of soft silk," says a Japanese proverb. The impalpable essence of Japanese patriotism takes the place of the soft strand in this instance. The divine origin of the Emperor, the unbroken line of his descent from the immortals, the guardianship that his deified ancestors extend to the realm and its people — these are essential bases of Japanese patriotism. It is a passionate patriotism, a fierce patriotism, overlaid from time to time in the past by ashes of disloyal ambition or domestic dissension, but now fanned into strong flame by the wind of Western masterfulness and intolerance.

Whether any Japanese subject could openly dissociate himself from the tenets of this national cult — for patriotism in modern Japan is nothing less than a national cult — and could yet lead a pleasant, peaceful existence, is at least problematical. At any rate, there has been no evident tendency towards dissociation. Some compromise seems to have been effected between conscience and convention. It must be added, also, that worship as a unit of a large company on the State occasions alluded to above, is not the only ordeal prescribed by custom. Any official, humble or exalted, who is ordered to proceed abroad on public business, must, before leaving Japan, proceed to the Hall of Reverence and perform an act of homage or worship, whichever definition he pleases to adopt. That is a duty: there is no option. Possibly it is regarded in the light merely of a farewell declaration of allegiance. Possibly, also, the main body of the Christians in Japan accept the subtle distinction privately drawn by some of their fellow-believers, that so long as there is no worship in spirit, genuflections performed by the body have no connection with religion. But it is singular that this question has always been excluded from the sphere of public discussion, and singular also that Christians do not apparently recognize how plainly they are differentiated

PREPARING A DINNER.

from the rest of the nation by the absence of any representative on ceremonial occasions in the Hall of Reverence. There is no native Christian prelate in Japan. There are Roman Catholic and Protestant hierarchs of European and American origin, — an archbishop and several bishops and archdeacons, — but as yet no Japanese subject has attained to such dignity. Each sect, however, has its senior pastor or father, of Japanese nationality, and unless these attend the ceremonials in the Hall of Reverence as do the chief representatives of Buddhism, the Christian element of the population continues to be marked as standing aloof from rites which, in the eyes of patriotic Japanese, are connected with the very basis of nationalism. We merely state the problem. It cannot be omitted from any record of the conditions existing in modern Japan.

The days set apart for these ceremonials within the palace are not marked by any act of general devotion without, since the Emperor worships in lieu of his people. They are merely observed as national holidays. Every householder hangs the national flag before his gate, but visits are not paid to temples or shrines, nor is there any other evidence of a special occasion. It should be noted, too, that the description given here applies only to the ceremonial system organized subsequently to the Restoration in 1867. Prior to that time, the deities supposed to preside over worldly affairs were worshipped at fifteen set seasons annually. But the rites have been reduced and simplified. Formerly, the deities that gave abundant crops; the deities that warded off plague and pestilence; the deities that breathed the spirit of vigor into things animate and inanimate; the deities that guarded against conflagrations; the deities that quelled evil demons; the deities that laid to rest wandering souls of the dead; the deities that made rain fall in time of drought — all these were severally and collectively placated. But now the *Shinto* of the State has made a large step toward monotheism. Amaterasu is worshipped as the supreme being; her descendants, the ancestors of the Emperor, receive homage as associated deities performing a special tutelary *rôle;* the other members of the pantheon are virtually neglected.

WEIGHING TEA.

This part of our subject would not be complete without a word about the *Shinto* shrines and Buddhist temples as they exist to-day.

Shrines are divided into four official grades — state, provincial, prefectural, and divisional or district. There are subdivisions to which we need not refer. State shrines are dedicated, for the most part, to the divine ancestors, but at a few the objects of worship are sovereigns or subjects that attained special distinction.[1] Between a state shrine of the first grade and a district shrine of the last, there is, of course, a great difference in standing, but there need not be any corresponding difference in the relative importance of the deities worshipped there. Sometimes the object of worship at a state shrine of most imposing character is venerated elsewhere under circumstances that suggest an altogether inferior being. It is simply a question of local repute, financial capabilities or other independent causes, just as in the Occident the same God is prayed to in city cathedrals and village churches. The shrine of the Sun Goddess, the *Daijin-gu* of Ise, stands at the head of all, but scarcely a hamlet in the realm is without a *Daijingu* of its own under the alias of *Myo-jin.* As for the number of the deities, it has never been counted by official statisticians. But the shrines that enjoy any considerable popularity are comparatively few, not more than

---

[1] It might be supposed that many Emperors would have received this distinction. But among the hundred and twenty-eight sovereigns who have sat on the throne of Japan, two only — Ojin and Kwammu — are thus honored. On the other hand, great subjects have been deified much more frequently; for example, Sugawara no Michizane (Temman), Kusunoki Masashige (Minatogawa), Tokugawa Ieyasu (Tosho), Hideyoshi the *Taiko* (Toyokuni), etc.

TATTOOED POSTMAN.

The art of tattooing is carried to great perfection in Japan and receives patronage from foreigners as well as natives. The mail carrier in the country districts of today, is sometimes clad in this picturesque but unsubstantial attire which in ancient times was regarded with universal favor. The packet containing the mail is attached to the end of a bamboo pole and carried on the shoulder.

ten in all. The incomes enjoyed by these shrines are not formidable. Some can boast of forty thousand *yen* annually; some of only a few hundred. Small grants from the State, supplemented by the offerings of the pious and the sale of amulets, are the sources of revenue. The special functions assigned by the people to the deities worshipped at these shrines are various. No one knows what spirit of heaven or earth is venerated at the *Suiten-gu* in Tokyo, and the shrine enjoys the peculiar distinction of being the private property of a nobleman. It stands within the precincts of his residence and contributes a handsome sum to his yearly maintenance. But despite the anonymity of the god, people credit him with power to protect against all perils of sea and flood, against burglary and, by a strange juxtaposition of "spheres of influence," against the pains of parturition. The deity of *Inari* secures efficacy for prayer and abundance of crops; the *Taisha* presides over wedlock; the *Kompira* shares with the *Suiten-gu* the privilege of guarding those that "go down to the deep." The rest confer prosperity, avert sickness, cure sterility, bestow literary talent, endow with warlike prowess, and so on. There are no less than 193,476 *Shinto* shrines in Japan, but 14,766 priests suffice to perform the rites of the creed. It will be asked how one priest manages to officiate at 13 shrines — which is the average. The answer is that he does not officiate, as folks in the West understand the term. It may be said generally of *Shinto* shrines that not more than one service is performed there annually. The building stands frequently uninhabited, apparently untended. Now and then a worshipper comes, grasps the thick hempen rope that hangs in front, sways it against the gong across which it is suspended, and having thus summoned the presiding spirit, mutters a brief prayer, deposits two or three *cash* in the alms chest and goes his way. The Buddhists have 108,000 temples and 55,000 priests. It will be seen that many of these temples cannot fare better in the matter of ministrations than do the *Shinto* shrines.

As *Shinto* shrines are officially graded, so are the priests' connected with them. But the rank held by the greatest of the latter corresponds only with that of a local governor or a Vice-Minister of State. The hierarchy does not climb to a lofty elevation; there is no Archbishop of Canterbury, no Pope of Rome. Nor would the emoluments of office excite the envy of an English rector. The official allowance, when there is one, varies from 100 *yen* to 33 *yen* monthly. Supplemented by a portion of the income accruing to the shrine, the portliest stipend of a *Shinto* priest probably amounts to twenty pounds sterling per month. In order to qualify for the magnificent chance of such opulence, he has to pass an examination, unless, indeed — and the contingency is not rare — his father and forefathers have been priests for ten generations. Buddhist priests have no official rank, nor are their temples graded. They live on the contributions of their parishioners and on the income derived from lands that were of great extent and large wealth-yielding capacity until the government of the Restoration reduced their area to a mere fraction of its original dimensions.

---

[1] It is not absolutely correct to speak of a *Shinto* minister as a "priest." He is called *Shinkwan*, which signifies rather a "*Shinto* official."

X.

SUPERSTITIONS AND DIVINATION.

THE middle and lower orders in Japan and women of all classes are undoubtedly superstitious. They believe in ghosts, in demons, in the possession of supernatural power by animals, in the efficacy of divination and in the potency of spells and amulets.

It seems curious at first sight that a people whose treatment of animals is markedly kind should regard the deity of the animal world as an inhuman monster, and should attribute one of the most terrible phenomena of nature as well as many of the accidents of daily life to the malevolent interference of fabulous creatures. It is popularly believed that a giant catfish (*namazu*) lies under Japan. Over its head is built the shrine of Daimyo-jin at Kashima in the province of Hitachi, and the deity is supposed to have his feet planted on the monster's snout. Whenever the god reduces the pressure or alters the position of his feet the catfish writhes and the earth quakes. Beside the shrine stands a stone called "the pivot rock" (*kaname-ishi*). It is in the form of a rude pillar, and the people believe that it penetrates to an enormous depth and reaches to the head of the catfish. But these theories are in some degree the outcome of a time when animals were actually a source of terror. Japan was never troubled, it is true, by the fiercer beasts of prey, lions and tigers, nor yet by venomous reptiles. If her island chain once formed a part of the Korean peninsula, as is generally believed, it would seem inevitable that the tiger should have made his home in Japanese forests no less than in Korean. But there is no evidence that either tiger or lion ever roamed the wilds of Japan. Snakes abound, but with one solitary exception — the *mamushi*--they are absolutely harmless. Wolves, however, were certainly numerous and destructive in ancient times, though they may now be said to survive in the realm of tradition only, and bears occasionally showed formidable propensities, though they, too, are to-day regarded merely as the hunter's quarry. At present the wild dog- the "mountain dog" (*yama-inu*)- is the only beast that inspires terror. He is not a wolf, but merely a dog that has never been domesticated. The Japanese dog is a miserable brute. In the stage of puppy-hood he presents some attractive features of fluffiness and rotundity, and artists have often recognized his picturesque qualities. But a few months of life suffice to convert him into an ill-shapen, unsightly and useless cur. Except with children, therefore, he is never a pet, and he requites their kindness by eating them. Even within the precincts of the capital, during recent years, packs of dogs, starving outcasts, have been known to pull down a child in one of the waste spaces that mark the sites of former feudal mansions. Little children, however, are now the only victims of such shocking accidents; whereas beasts of prey were formerly terrible to adults also, as may be inferred from a cruel custom, long abandoned indeed but certainly practised in remote eras, the custom of offering human sacrifices to the deity of animals. Tradition has become much confused about this custom. Many Japanese believe that human beings were among the offerings originally made to the tutelary deities in conjunction with fish, vegetables and products of industry. But the best authorities agree that such sacrifices were made to the god of wild beasts only. The victim was always a girl, and the manner of selecting her was singular. From the earliest ages the archer's weapons have been regarded with the utmost reverence in Japan. Having been originally instrumental in bringing the barbarous autochthons under the celestial invaders' sway, the bow and the arrow subsequently became symbols of security against all perils, and in that sense were fixed upon the ridge-pole of a newly erected roof. The habit survives still. Not in remote country districts only, but even in the great cities, houses may to-day be seen

SAMURAI IN ARMOR.
The weapon with a long handle is a glaive.

with a bent bow and an adjusted arrow standing where a chimney would protrude its head from a Western roof. It is said that, in prehistoric times, the bow and arrow assumed that position by an exercise of supernatural power. A householder, rising in the morning, would find that his roof had been thus distinguished during the night, and the event was accepted as a divine intimation that the eldest unmarried daughter of the family must be sacrificed. She was buried alive, the supposition being that her flesh served as a repast for the deity. But the priests by and by found a more profitable manner of disposing of these unfortunate girls: they were sold as slaves. The tradition is a mixed record of practical knavery and gross superstition. The bow-and-arrow sign plainly indicates that rustic ignorance was exploited by dishonest priests. On the other hand, the superstitious fancy must have existed or it could not have been played upon. There is little hope, apparently, of ascertaining the details of a custom which probably ceased to be practical before the first records of popular life were compiled.[1]

Another form of human sacrifice believed to have been common in early ages and said to have been witnessed by men of the present generation was called *ikiuzume*, or burying alive. The prevalent idea about this custom is that, at the inception of some great work, such as the building of a bridge or the erection of a castle, a human being was buried alive near the foundations to secure stability. But facts and fancies are here commingled. What really happened was this: In the era of forced labor, when every adult rustic had to contribute a certain number of days' work annually to the service of the State or of his liege lord, it was usual for the official superintendent of these unwilling toilers to stand over them with a bare-bladed spear in hand. Any display of laziness justified fatal recourse to the spear, and the corpse of a man thus done to death was treated as so much inanimate material — thrown between the piles of an embankment or tossed into the foundations of a building. That species of fierce incitement was generally resorted to when extraordinary expedition had to be attained: when an inundation had to be averted, a river dammed before the flowing of the tide, a fortification constructed on the eve of attack, or a work concluded in anticipation of the advent of some great man. It proved, of course, immensely efficacious, and may serve in some degree to explain the really wonderful achievements that stand to the credit of human effort in mediæval and even in modern Japan. Two corpses are said to be mouldering under the scarps of the futile forts hurriedly erected for the defence of Edo (Tokyo) in the interval between Commodore Perry's first and second comings; and looking down from Noge Hill in the suburbs of Yokohama one may see the shrine of a servant girl who sacrificed herself to expedite the reclamation of a swamp behind the foreign settlement. Such incidents, however, had not in their origin any legitimate connection with superstition.

Since the English word " nightmare " indicates that the subjective character of that natural disturbance was not recognized when the Anglo-Saxon language came into existence, we are prepared to find a corresponding superstition among the Japanese. They used to believe, and the lower orders do still believe, that a rat possesses some demoniacal power which it exercises maliciously during the night. But nobody concerns himself much about the question. Half a page of history, however, is devoted to the account of an Imperial nightmare, the work of a very strange monster. The Emperor Shirakawa the second (1153 A. D.) was the victim of the visitation. Every night he fell into convulsions, and neither medicine nor prayer gave him relief. It was observed that, at the moment of his seizure, a dark cloud emerged from a forest eastward of the palace and settled over the roof of his

[1] The monster at whose shrine these sacrifices (*htomigoku*, literally, offerings of a human body) are said to have been made, is spoken of by some writers as an animal in the service of Sâkyamuni. The responsibility of the barbarous rite would therefore rest with Buddhism. But the sanctity of life has always been a fundamental tenet of the Buddhist religion. Thus the tradition becomes altogether vague and untrustworthy as to its details. Nothing can be accepted as certain except the fact that human sacrifices were made to propitiate the deity of wild beasts, and that human beasts subsequently turned the superstition to their own villanous uses.

majesty's chamber. The court, in conclave, decided that a warrior's weapon was needed, and invited the renowned Yorimasa to undertake the task. That night, as the cloud floated to its place and the Emperor's paroxysm overtook him, Yorimasa, with a prayer to *Hachiman* (the God of War) on his lips, shot an arrow into the heart of the cloud. There fell to the ground a monster with the head of an ape, the body of a serpent, the legs of a tiger and the strident cry of the fabulous bird *nue*. Yorimasa received as reward an Imperial sword and a palace maiden, and the Emperor's nightmares ceased. There could be no doubt in the minds of later generations about the accuracy of these facts, for even the name of the beautiful girl bestowed on Yorimasa was known : it was " Sweet-flag" (*Ayame*). Such a detail raised the record to the rank of authentic history in the eyes of people who believed the wind to be the breath of a mighty spirit and the stars to be the sources of rain-drops.

Among all superstitions connected with animals in Japan, faith in the supernatural attributes of the fox is most widely entertained. This notion was originally imported from China. The fox, according to popular tradition, can assume human form, and is also capable of entering into a man or woman. Roaming over a grassy plain, the animal picks up a skull, puts it on his head, and facing towards the north star, worships. At first he performs his religious genuflections and obeisances slowly and circumspectly, but by and by, however high he jumps towards the star, his skull-crown remains immovable. After a hundred acts of worship, he becomes capable of transforming himself into a human being; but if he desires to be able to assume the shape of a beautiful maiden, he must live in the vicinity of a grave-yard. As a girl he is the central figure in numerous legends. His very name — *ki-tsu-ne* " come and sleep" — is derived from such a legend, a white-haired legend of the year 545

WRECKED BY AN EARTHQUAKE.

A. D. Ono, an inhabitant of Mino, spent the seasons longing for his ideal of female beauty. He met her one evening on a vast moor and married her. Simultaneously with the birth of their son, Ono's dog was delivered of a pup, which, as it grew up, became more and more hostile to the lady of the moors. She begged her husband to kill it, but he refused. At last, one day, the dog attacked her so fiercely that she lost heart, resumed her proper shape, leaped over the fence and fled. "You may be a fox," Ono called after her, " but you are the mother of my son and I love you. Come back when you please; you will always be welcome." So every evening she stole back and slept in his arms. The illiterate Japanese, even of the present

KIGA ROAD NEAR MIYANOSHITA.

day, though he may not entertain any very positive faith in such occurrences, preserves toward them a demeanor of respectful uncertainty. There are scores of such stories, and hundreds of folks who listen to them gravely. There are also weak-minded persons to whose imagination these legends appeal so vividly that they become subjective victims of fox-possession. They bark like a fox, exhibit the utmost aversion to dogs and otherwise lose their human identity. In many cases these imaginary seizures are cured by the aid of a priest. The patient is informed that means of enticing the fox to return to the hills have been provided, and that, at a certain hour and in obedience to a religious incantation, the animal will take its departure. Such remedies, attended, as they generally are, by success, have the effect of confirming the superstition ; and in rural districts few Japanese are entirely without belief in the phenomenon of fox-possession (*kitsune-tsuki*). History is not without records attesting the supernatural powers of the fox. On the Nasu moor (*Nasu-no hara*) in the province of Shimotsuke there used to stand a large rock known as *sessho-seki*, or the stone of death. It had been bewitched by a fox, and any living thing that touched it, man, bird or animal, perished. In the year 1248 the Emperor Fukakusa II commissioned a priest of renowned piety, Genno Osho, to exorcise the evil spirit. Genno repaired to the moor, invoked the aid of Buddha and struck the rock with his staff, whereupon the big stone split into fragments, and a beautiful girl stepping out, thanked the priest with tears and vanished.

The badger (*tanuki*) is credited with somewhat similar powers, but is regarded rather as a mischievous practical joker than as a malicious demon. One of his most celebrated exploits as a supernatural trickster was in connection with a tea-urn which fell into the uncanny habit of developing the tail, snout and claws of a badger at most inopportune moments of a social reunion. On moonlight nights the badger raises himself on his hind legs and goes roistering about the country, beating upon his paunch as though it were a drum, knocking at the doors of timid folks, leading belated travellers into wrong roads and terrifying children and old women in sundry ways. The house of a farmer in the province of Awa recently became the beast's playground. A kitchen knife moved automatically from peg to block, and the fish-kettle was found to contain only boiling water when meal time arrived. One day a rustic presented himself as the servant of a man to whom the farmer owed money and demanded payment in his master's name. The farmer handed over three pieces of silver. After a time the creditor himself came and asked for his money. Then, of course, the farmer knew that he had been tricked by a badger. Presently the tail of the farm horse was shorn off by invisible agency, and the horse itself, escaping from the stable, took refuge in a neighboring village. The farmer led it back, locked it in and locked the badger out, but again the horse absconded, and on searching its stall the farmer found the three pieces of silver that had been carried off by the pseudo servant. In such *rôles* the badger thrusts himself upon the stage of human existence. His sphere of influence is occasionally invaded by the sickle-bearing demon, *kama-itachi*, a nondescript demon which sometimes cuts tresses from women's hair as they walk in unfrequented places, and often inflicts bleeding wounds on people's legs and arms without any visible exercise of effort. The *kama-itachi's* performances are vaguely connected with a sudden solution of atmospheric continuity, a whirlwind or other aerial disturbance; and if a country bumpkin finds that he has unconsciously received a hurt, he has no hesitation in attributing it to the demoniacal sickle-carrier. The *kappa* (river-urchin) is another fabulous monster, malevolent like the sickle-bearer, but more deadly

NAKAJIMA, NAGASAKI.

in its doings. It dwells in rivers and lakes, and its favorite haunts are catalogued with solemn accuracy. No one has attempted to describe the *kama-itachi*, but the *kappa's* appearance is minutely depicted. It has the body of a ten-year-old child, is hairy like a monkey, possesses eyes of piercing brilliancy, has in its skull a cup-like cavity, speaks the language of human beings, lives in the water, but emerges at nightfall and steals melons and egg-fruit, its favorite food. Wrestling is the pastime affected by it. It invites men to try a bout, and despite its puny proportions, comes off violently victorious, unless, indeed, the water contained in its skull-cap be spilled, when its strength vanishes. To defeat it, however, is as bad as to be defeated, for the result is loss of reason and gradual wasting away. This river-urchin, in common with the snapping-turtle, is credited with vampire propensities; it attacks people in the water and sucks their blood.[1] Even the dog has a place in Japanese demonology. How the faithful animal originally fell under suspicion of supernatural wickedness it is difficult to ascertain, but tradition represents him not as naturally malevolent, but merely as the agent of human passion. An old woman consumed with hatred of a powerful enemy whom her vengeance could not reach, buried her favorite dog in the ground so that its head alone protruded, and then, having fondled the head for a time, cut it off with a bamboo saw, saying: "If you have a soul, kill my enemy, and I will worship you as a deity." Her wish was gratified, but the spirit of the dog became thenceforth an inmate of her house and made her suffer for her cruelty.[2] The superstition outlined by this legend generally takes the form of a belief that the blood of the dog-demon (*inu-gami*) flows in the veins of certain families. In the "island of the four provinces" (*Shikoku*) and in the eight provinces forming the "mountain-shadow district" (*San-in-dō*), the dog-demon is supposed to have tainted many households, and ignorant folks, before contracting a marriage, are careful to employ an expert who examines the genealogical tables of the bride and bridegroom in order to ascertain whether they contain any trace of the evil influence. Bakin, Japan's greatest writer of fiction, based his celebrated romance, the "eight-dog tale" (*Hakken-den*), upon the Buddhist doctrine that animals have souls. Frequently characteristic of fox-possessed men is an outrageous insistence on being served with the best of everything at the shortest notice, but when any one lineally related to the dog-demon covets the possessions of a neighbor, the influence of the *inu-gami* overtakes the latter and quickly reduces him to a state of dementia.

It will readily be conceived that if the dog finds a place in demonology, the cat is not exempted. The latter, indeed, figures prominently in some most aristocratic legends, and is made responsible for crimes which, under less romantic circumstances, would be ascribed to very vulgar passions. Old age develops the cat's evil propensities. When time has rendered it gaunt and grisly it becomes a *neko-mata*, or cat-imp. Its agency is detected in weird lights that dance above the floor, darting out of reach when pursued, in the spinning of untouched wheels, in the turning of beds during their inmates' sleep. Then, perhaps, the

---

[1] In the Uma district of Iyo province there is a lake where country folk often bathe in the dog days. There the river-urchin or the snapping-turtle is said to claim two victims yearly. They lose their color after emerging from the lake, and gradually pine away with symptoms that do not bear description.

[2] The example set by this vengeful old woman is said to have been followed by others in a more logical fashion. Their idea being to convert the spirit of longing into a physical agency, they buried a dog, leaving only its head exposed, and surrounding it with tempting viands, suffered it to starve to death. Having thus received a vivid object lesson in the pain of unsatisfied desire, the dog's spirit was supplicated to save its former master or mistress from similar suffering.

old cat is detected sitting on its hind legs with its head wrapped in the towel of the person it intends to bewitch, and if it is killed opportunely, it is found to have two tails and a body five feet long.

Among people so profoundly convinced of the truth of animistic philosophy and, at the same time, so keenly appreciative of the beauties of nature, it was inevitable that the most graceful or brilliant objects in the world of foliage and flowers should be invested with spirit attributes. Many pretty legends grew out of that conviction. The cherry bloom, type of glowing loveliness, and the willow, image of everything that is refined and gentle, often took the shape of winsome maidens and bestowed themselves upon some great warrior or noble exile. So, too, when Suguwara-no-Michizane, the most worthy and the most unfortunate of Japanese statesmen, became the victim of a rival's slanders and was banished to Dazaifu in Chikuzen, the rosy-petalled plum tree on whose boughs he had hung verselets every spring from the days of his boyhood, flew through the clouds from Kyoto and planted itself by his side in the place of his solitude. The Japanese love this legend of the flying plum (*tobi-ume*), and love also to tell of the peonies of Ono-no-komachi, the celebrated

PEASANT WOMAN CARRYING FAGOTS.

poetess, whose life included the most luxurious and the most illustrious, as well as the most miserable and the most abject experiences that ever fell to the lot of an Oriental lady. In the village where she was born a shrine stands dedicated to her memory, and near it grow ninety-nine peony trees, planted by her own hand just a thousand years ago, and now tended by her spirit. From time to time some of the little trees were transplanted for the sake of their magnificent blossoms, to city gardens, but invariably they pined away and would have perished had they not been carried back to their old place beside the shrine.

Buddhism, with its worlds of hungry devils and of infernal beings and its realistic pictures of the torments suffered by the souls of men in Yemma's (the god of Hades) kingdom, is responsible for the Japanese people's conception of an anthropomorphic demon (*oni*). They represent him with horns, a vast, heavy-fanged mouth, glaring eyes, a flat nose, broadly expanding nostrils, three-fingered hands and three-toed feet, long silvery talons, and wearing nothing but a girdle of tiger skin. He has all the ferocity and all the malignity proper to his kind. He takes his pastime when on earth in the depths of forests and the caverns of remote mountains, lives there on human flesh and carries off beautiful women to share his orgies. In the ninth century he began to be a prominent figure in Japanese imagination, and his doings since that era are recorded in a library of startling records too voluminous to be opened here. There is, however, another genus of demon that deserves notice as being essentially an outcome of Japanese fancy. It is the *tengu*,[1] a monster of huge stature and enormous strength, with the body of a man and the face and wings of a bird. The demon proper (*oni*) has his permanent abode in other worlds, but the *tengu* is still supposed to frequent the recesses of high mountains. He is not a particularly malevolent being. Sometimes he spirits men away and restores them to their homes in a semi-demented condition; sometimes he enters into frail girls and endows them with martial prowess of a miraculous quality; sometimes he gives fencing lessons to future heroes.[2] But he has faded, for the most part, out of the vista of adult observation, and now figures chiefly in children's tales and old women's fables.

Believing that the spirits of the dead watch over and protect their living kindred, the Japanese believe also that the ghosts of the departed sometimes vex and torture those who used them ill on this side of the grave. Deeds of blood and cruelty have brought upon their perpetrators apparitions and mental torments ending in madness, ruined fortunes and suicide. The lower orders found comfort in thinking that the miseries they had sometimes to suffer unresistingly at the hands of the great, might be thus requited after the death of the sufferer, but, on the whole, the restless ghost with a mission of revenge never seriously disturbed the public mind. Haunted houses, however, are so common that in every city two or three may be seen standing untenanted. Educated men might have no hesitation in renting or purchasing such places, but they would certainly find difficulty in getting servants to live there, from which it may be inferred that the reality of ghostly appearances is not questioned by the masses. When a girl warns her faithless lover that her spirit will haunt him (*tottsuku*), she does not doubt her ability to make the threat good, and when folks allege that they have seen the soul of the newly dead float away over eaves and roof, a transparent globe[3] of impalpable

---

[1] The *tengu* is one of the most mysterious of Japanese monsters. The ideographs with which the name is written signify "heavenly dog." One tradition says that, in the year 638 A. D., the Emperor Jomyo gave the name *tengu* to a meteor which flashed from east to west with a loud detonation. Another and more venerable account alleges that the *tengu* were emanations from the excessive ardor of the " Impetuous Male Deity " (Susa-no-o) ; that they were female demons, with human bodies, beasts' heads, vast ears, noses so long that they could hang men on them and fly a thousand miles without feeling the burden, teeth that bit through swords and spears, and the faculty of becoming pregnant by inhaling miasma. They defy the control of the celestial deities and are altogether an unruly, tameless band. The description of the *tengu* given in the text is, however, the popularly received idea.

[2] Yoshitsune, the hero of the *Gem-pei* wars in the thirteenth century, is supposed to have received fencing lessons from a *tengu* in the woods near the monastery where his boyhood was passed.

[3] This phenomenon, spoken of as *hito-dama*, commands wide credence.

WISTARIA AT KAMEIDO TEMPLE, TOKYO.

The Shinto temple of Temmangu, commonly known as Kameido, is one of the chief show-places of the capital during the last week of April, when the wistaria in the temple grounds is in full blossom. It grows on the borders of a pond called *Shinji no Ike*, or "Pond of the Word Heart," on account of a resemblance between the form of the pond and the Chinese character signifying "heart."

essence, their faith in the accuracy of their eyesight is honest. Death is not an essential preliminary to the exercise of spirit power. The passion of hatred or revenge may become so intense as to liberate the soul from its bodily tenement, and despatch it upon a mission of hostility. All these beliefs have left their mark upon the literature of the nation and upon the canvas of the artist. In a deeper stratum of superstition may be found still stranger fossils of tradition — the wild man, the wild [1] woman, the female ogre (*kijo*) and the mountain genius (*sen-nin*). The wild man and the wild woman are harmless curiosities. There is a story of a wild woman caught in a spring trap in Hiuga province. Her body differed from that of an ordinary female only in being covered with white hair. The wild man is said to abound among the mountains of Kiushu, where the people call him *yama-waro*. He is described as a large, black-haired monkey, possessing enormous muscular strength. He steals food from the villages, but is always ready to help woodcutters to transport timber in return for a ball of rice. Any attempt to capture or kill him brings dire calamity, insanity, plague or sudden death upon his assailants. The female ogre (*kijo*) figures frequently in the pages of romance. She is a cannibal, capable of flitting about like a moth and traversing pathless mountains. Once in every cycle of sixty years, when the "senior fire element" is linked with the zodiacal horse, a female man-eater is born, but it does not follow that the intervening years are never disgraced by the appearance of such monsters, which, for the rest, belong rather

to the fantasies of the nursery than to the superstitions of grown-up folks. A more widely disseminated belief, which has also left indelible traces in the realm of fine art and sculpture, is based upon the theory that, by mortification of the flesh and complete annihilation of all carnal desires, the divine attributes of the soul may be actively developed though it still

SANMAI BASHI TEA HOUSE.

retains its earthly tenement. This superstition came to Japan from China. It had its origin in the hermits or ascetics who hid themselves in mountain caves beyond the sounds of the world's passion and confusion, and thus, fading imperceptibly out of human knowledge, were

[1] Literally the "mountain man" (*yama-otoko*) and the "mountain woman" (*yama-onna*).

supposed to have attained immortality. These *sen-nin*, or genii of the mountains, found imitators in Japan, as did everything Chinese. Even now there are recluses living in hollow trees or rocky caverns among the forests and mountains of Ehime prefecture and of northern *Tosan-do*. They subsist on herbs and fruits, and hunters sometimes carry to country hamlets tales of strange beings appearing and disappearing so suddenly as to suggest supernatural powers. Out of such materials the myths of the *sen-nin*, and probably of the *ten-gu* also, were constructed. The Japanese view the *sen-nin* (or *rishi*) with playful gravity. In the innumerable representations of these strange beings that are to be found among the works of celebrated painters or carvers in wood and ivory, a ray of laughter always lightens the general austerity of the conception. Sobu, watching his sacred geese, looks as though he were himself on the verge of cackling; Chokaro, liberating his magic horse from a monster gourd, seems astounded at his own achievement; Gama, with his toad warlock, is sufficiently dirty, distraught and unkempt to suit such companionship; Tekkai, as he blows his soul into space, presents an inane aspect quite in character with the myth that he forgot to provide for the safety of his body during the wanderings of his spirit, and thus had to be ultimately content with the unburied corpse of a beggar; Roko balances himself on his flying tortoise with the air of a decrepit acrobat; and *Kumé*, who fell from his cloud-chariot because his carnal desires were revived by the sight of a beautiful girl's image mirrored in a stream, has a wavering mien suggestive of some such catastrophe. The mountain genii of Japan never meddled with earthly affairs, nor placed their supernatural powers at the disposal of human beings.

People to whose imagination the unknown fate of a hermit or the fanaticism of an ascetic presented such a mine of vivid myths did not fail to find weird explanations of the *ignis fatuus*. It was a ghost-fire (*in-kwa*), a demon-light (*oni-bi*), a fox-flame (*kitsune-bi*), a flash-pillar (*hibashira*), a badger-blaze (*tanuki-bi*), a dragon-torch (*riu-to*), a lamp of Buddha (*Butsu-to*), and so forth. Here are two of the legends that have grown out of these wild-fires:

In the Nikaido district of Settsu province, from the middle of March to the end of June every year, there may be seen, resting sometimes on a roof, sometimes on the top of a tree, a globe of fire about a foot in diameter, which, when examined intently, is found to have a human face peering from its lurid surface. It is a harmless phenomenon. The people regard it with pity, recalling its origin. For, in remote ages, there lived in this district one Nikōbō, a beadsman (*yamabushi*), celebrated for his skill in exorcism. His services having

---

[1] The first Japanese *sen-nin* was a native of Noto, by name Yōshō. He was born in 870 A. D., and his supernatural character was presaged by his mother's dream that she had swallowed the sun. Exceptional ability and profound charity marked his early life, which was devoted chiefly to the study of the "Lotus of the Law." Abstaining from rice and barley, he lived on fruit only, and at length he succeeded in reducing his diet to a grain of millet daily. Thus, having attained supernatural power, he departed from the earth in the year 901. His mantle was found hanging from the branch of a tree, with a scroll: — "I bequeath my mantle to Emmei of *Dōgen-ji*" (the name of a temple). Emmei, seeking his master year after year among forests and mountains, became himself a *sen-nin*. After Yōshō's disappearance, his father fell sick, and prayed fervently that he might once more see his favorite son. By and by the voice of Yōshō was heard overhead, reciting the "Lotus of the Law," and promising that if flowers were offered and incense burned on the 18th of every month, his spirit would come, drawn by the perfume and the flame, to requite his father's love.

been solicited on behalf of the sick wife of the local governor, he passed many days by the side of the lady's couch, practising his pious art. She recovered, but her husband in an excess of jealousy caused Nikôbô to be put to death, charging him with a foul crime. His benevolent work thus requited with inhuman wrong, the soul of the beadsman flamed with resentment, and taking the form of a miraculous fire, hovered over the roof of the murderer's house and kindled a fever in his blood that finally consumed him. Since that time Nikôbô's ghost-flame pays a yearly visit to the scene of its suffering and its revenge.

At the base of the Katada Hills in Omi province there lies a lake from whose margin on cloudy nights in early

LEARNING TO WRITE.

autumn a little ball of fire emerges. Creeping toward the feet of the mountains it grows as it goes, sometimes swelling to a brilliant sphere three feet in diameter, sometimes not developing to more than a third of that size, but always, when it rises to the height of a man's stature above the ground, showing within its glow two faces, to which gradually the torsos of two naked wrestlers, struggling furiously, attach themselves. It takes its way slowly and harmlessly to the recesses of the hills, but resents with superhuman force any attempt to interrupt its progress. Once, a wrestler of unconquered fame waited at midnight for its coming, and sprang to grasp it as it passed through the mists. He was hurled to a distance of ten or twelve yards, and barely escaped with his life.

Of the "badger-blaze" it is related that it wanders in the Kawabe district of Settsu on rainy nights, and that uninitiated rustics, mistaking it for the glowing pipe of an ox-driver, hold converse with the badger, who is at all times a sociable fellow, and have even lit their own tobacco at his and puffed it in his company. The numerous legends that Japanese fancy has woven around the will-o'-the-wisp have an interest of their own as illustrating the genius of the people, but our limits of space forbid fuller reference to the subject.

What has thus far been written about superstitions will have probably prepared the reader to hear that the Japanese have always been disposed to attach great importance to divination. It is unquestionable that Confucianism is largely responsible for the growth and persistence of such an irrational mood. So much time and study did the Chinese sage devote to the Book of Changes (*Yih King*) that the leather thongs holding its leaves together were worn out thrice during his lifetime. The result of his labors, as has been well said, was "to add some inexplicable chapters to an incomprehensible book." This *Yih King* has long been the chief vehicle for divination in Japan. Much of its supposed value lies in the mystery that enshrouds it. Starting from the fundamental idea that the universe had its origin in the union of the male and female principles, the *yin* and the *yang*, it undertakes to elaborate a theory of all physical phenomena and of all moral and political doctrines by means of eight trigrams and sixty-four diagrams. To attempt any full explanation of it would be to supplement vagueness by bewilderment. Chinese literati and foreign students alike having failed to understand it, we may fairly assume that it defies understanding. One point only may be noted, that as the evolution of written ideas in China could be traced in the growth of ideographs, which were simply linear combinations, partly systematic, partly arbitrary, so the authors[1] of the *Yih King*, when they sat down to ruminate on the processes of nature and the operations of the intellect, instinctively turned to the grouping of long and short lines as a vehicle for the construction of philosophical formulæ. If the mystical numbers in which Pythagoras sought the elements of realities had been themselves necessarily resolvable into lines, it is probable that he too would have shaped his fancies into diagrams and trigrams instead of expressing them in numerals. Thus much premised, we pass at once to an explanation of the simplest manner of divination, as prescribed by the *Yih King*,[2] since by following the process a tolerably clear idea is obtained of the manner in which the sexual principle and the trigrams serve for purposes of prediction. The Japanese have a very pithy proverb, *ataru mo hakke, ataranu mo hakke*, which means that the eight trigrams (*hakke*) are right and the eight trigrams are wrong; in other words, that the chances are even as to the worth or worthlessness of divination. But it is not to be denied that the faith of an immense number of people is belied by such an aphorism, and that failures to obtain true glimpses of the future by means of divining rods are generally attributed not so much to inefficacy in the doctrine as to imperfections in the mood of the disciple. The so-called "orthodox" and "intermediate" methods are altogether too complicated to be explained here, but the "abridged" is comparatively easy. It matters little, indeed, which method is employed so far as the method itself is concerned, but since everything depends on the singleness of the diviner's mind and the fervor of his faith, and since ordinary men cannot hope to abstract themselves completely from their environment for any lengthy period, the quickest process is the most likely to give good results. The diviner, having thoroughly cleansed his body, seats himself perfectly upright in a secluded chamber and reverentially grasps the fifty divining

[1] The Yih King was commenced by Fuh-hsi, thirty centuries before Christ, carried far toward completion by Wan Wang eighteen centuries later, and added to by Confucius.

[2] The Japanese call the book *Yě-ki*, and the method of divination derived from it *boku-zei* or *boku-zeichiku*; *boku* signifying divination; *zei* and *chiku*, respectively, *lespedeza sericea* and bamboo, of which woods the divining sticks are made.

rods, remembering always that they are sacred media through which the purposes of the all-powerful are revealed by the aid of certain numerical mutations. One of the rods—any one—is separated from the rest and set upright in the rod-rack, thus becoming the "great origin." The lower ends of the remaining rods are then held with the left hand and their upper ends are slightly dovetailed. With the right hand, thumb inside, fingers outside, the forty-nine rods are now raised above the head. This is the supreme moment. The eyes are closed, the respiration is suspended, the thoughts are concentrated solemnly on the almighty intervention about to be invoked. Presently the senses are pervaded by a thrill indicating that communication with the supernatural has been established, and at that instant the rods are divided into two groups, the celestial and the terrestrial, the "positive" and the "negative." The right-hand group is laid on the table, and one rod having been removed from it,

is inserted lengthways between the third and little fingers of the left hand, the figure thus formed being a trigram, "heaven, earth and mankind." The left-hand group is then counted in cycles of eight two by two— and the remainder, including the rod held between the third and little fingers, is noted. Evidently there may be any remainder from 0 to 7, and these eight possibilities commencing with unity and ending with cipher correspond to eight trigrams representing "heaven," "morass," "fire," "thunder," "wind," "water," "mountain" and "earth." The trigram indicated by the remainder is called the "inner complement," and is placed at the bottom of the group which, when completed, will give the desired information. The above process is now repeated and a second trigram is obtained. It is called the "outer complement," and being placed at the top of the projected group, gives, with the "inner complement," a diagram of six lines, which has its corresponding ideograph. The rods are

EN DÉSHABILLÉ.

now once more divided and again counted, this time in cycles of six, and from the remainder another trigram is obtained. Thus gradually a diagram of six trigrams is built up, and from the pages of the *Yih King* used after the manner of a dictionary, the corresponding interpretation is taken out.

Professors of this art of divination are numerous,[1] their clients legion. The great adepts live in imposing mansions; the rank and file are content to spread a mat by the roadside, and there with conspicuously disposed paraphernalia of rods and tomes await the casual consultations that timid or bashful folk are glad to hold. The fee varies from two or three *sen* to a *yen*, and in cases of importance very much larger sums are paid. It will readily be conceived that many other systems of vaticination are practised. Two,[2] which find considerable vogue, may be roughly described as the casting of horoscopes. Both are primarily based on the assumption that every human being has received from heaven a vital essence, or spirit (*ki*), by the influence of which his health, his conduct and his moral ability are determined. The hour, the day, the month and the year of a man's birth, when expressed in terms of the elementary and zodiacal series, furnish materials for constructing a horoscope, from which the course of procedure best adapted to the nature of this "spirit" may be mapped out. Thus these forms of divination do not aim so much at furnishing exact predictions as at developing the better side of a man's character and enabling him to avert calamities which the preponderance of his inferior elements would certainly entail. Men of means and position and students on the threshold of independent life or struggling to win academical laurels, have recourse to adepts in these systems, which they regard as more or less useful guides to moral philosophy. The exact methods pursued by a professor in analyzing the "prime essence" of an inquirer cannot be defined, the processes of the art being known only to the families in which they have been secretly transmitted from generation to generation and by whose representatives they are practised. Physiognomy (*kwan-so*)[3] constitutes a serviceable but not an essential assistant, the vital indications being drawn from the horoscope.

Considered from the point of view of the large part that it plays in the every-day life of the people, the system of "aspect divination" (*hōi-jutsu*) is more important than any of the above. It is a species of astrology based upon the supposition that the supernatural influences which mould a man's destiny emanate from certain regions of the starry firmament, and that good is invited or evil averted by turning toward the auspicious quarter or away from the inauspicious at critical seasons in life. The Gregorian calendar was finally adopted in Japan thirty years ago, but the two series of "terrestrial stems" and "celestial branches" out of which the cycles of the old almanac were constructed, still present to the astrologer and horoscopist ready means of establishing connections between any point of the compass and the date of a birth, and nothing then remains except to assign special attributes to special stars or combinations of stars. It would appear that in remote ages this theory had not

---

[1] In Tokyo the most famous are Sekirushi (in Shiba district), Chieda (in Asakusa district) and Kishima and Sato (in Shitaya district).

[2] The *Ten-gen* (heavenly original) and the *In-kiu* (zodiacal essence system). The former was introduced from China in the year 960 A. D.: the latter is a Japanese modification of the former, dating from 1835. A third and cognate system, known as *Kanshi-jutsu* (the element and zodiacal art), is of somewhat later origin than the *In-kiu*. Among living representatives of the *To-kiu* are the widows of two of its formerly renowned professors, and it receives large support from the noble families of Suwa and Tachibana.

[3] Called also *Ninso-jutsu*, and practised as an independent science.

emerged from a rudimentary form. Men believed that somewhere away in the northeast stood the demons' gate (*ki-mon*) and that human beings should preserve toward that quarter a demeanor of reverential deprecation- should not face it in sleeping, should not turn their feet thitherward at the commencement of a journey, should not give their houses a north-easterly aspect, should not cultivate the corner of their parks or gardens on which the eyes of the evil spirits looked out from the portals of bad omen. The celebrated monastery of Hiei-zan on the northeast of the Imperial palace in Kyoto, and the scarcely less celebrated temples of Uyeno on the northeast of the *Shogun's* palace in Tokyo, were religious barriers suggested by this superstition; and if any one examines the pleasure grounds surrounding Japanese houses, he will see that the northeasterly quarter is always thickly planted and left without ornamental rockery or invading path. Such evidences of practical demonology afford, how-ever, but a slight glimpse of the importance attached by the middle and lower classes, and even by many members of the upper, to the question of celestial quarter. Oshima Sekibun, the chief professor of the science of "aspect divination," is unable, even with the aid of a large band of disciples to furnish oracles for the multitudes that come daily to consult him. There are numbers of sober business men and educated gentlemen in Tokyo—to say nothing of the softer sex and the ignorant—who deem it absolutely essential to preface every important act by recourse to this kind of augury. Before building a house, before selecting a site, before changing from one residence to another, before opening a store, before applying for an official post, before engaging in any industrial or commercial enterprise, before betrothing a son or daughter, before fixing the date of a marriage, before despatching a cargo, before setting out on a journey, before preparing for an accouchement, before any of these things, and, in the case of the more superstitious, before any act that lies outside the most ordinary routine of every-day existence, the advice of the aspect diviner has to be sought.[1]

Prominence has here been given to modes of divination which may still be classed among the important customs of the nation. But others of great interest, though now more or less obsolete, deserve passing notice. Among these the oldest appears to have been scapulimancy, or divining by the cracks and lines in the scorched shoulder blade of a deer. It is suggestive that the same method of discerning the future was practised in ancient times in Tartary, Mongolia, Arabia, Lapland and even England,- (known as "reading the spealbone").

[1] A Tokyo newspaper recently published a statement illustrating the uses to which diviners are put. A man having purchased a quantity of vegetables, hired a cart for their transport. Needing to make a diversion from the direct route homeward, he bade the carter wait at a certain place. The carter seized the opportunity to abscond with the vegetables. When their owner discovered his loss he repaired to the house of a diviner, obtained information as to the whereabouts of the thief, and hastening off, apprehended him in the act of selling the vege-tables. Another story of contemporary doings shows the adroitness of the diviners in accounting for their failures. A person in good circum-stances learned from a horoscopist the exact date of his death. He regulated his affairs accordingly, spent his money lavishly, and having procured a coffin and paid his funeral expenses, lay down to await the supreme moment. It came and passed uneventfully. He therefore pro-ceeded to upbraid the diviner. The latter listened calmly to his reproaches and finally asked : "May I inquire whether you devoted any of your fortune to charitable objects?" "Certainly," replied the other. "Believing that my opportunities of spending money were brief, I gave away considerable sums in that way." "Just so," said the diviner. "But you failed to observe that benevolent deeds establish a claim upon heaven's protection, and that they would surely be rewarded by the lengthening of your life."

Tortoise-shell was subsequently substituted for shoulder-bones, a change especially convenient for women, who, by burning the ends of their tortoise-shell combs and observing the divergence or convergence, regularity or confusion, of the lines on the charred surface, drew inferences about the course of their love affairs. Another method, much practised by girls, was to stand by the roadside in the evening and construct auguries by patching together such fragments of wayfarers' talk as were wafted to their ears. This *tsugi-ura*, or road divining, has quite gone out of vogue. The term is now applied to mottoes placed within envelopes of sweet biscuit, after the "cracker" fashion of the West. But in former days the doubts of the heartsick were often resolved and the aspirations of the village belle encouraged by such glimpses of fate's purposes. Sometimes a rod was planted in the ground to personify the deity of roads—the god formed from Izanagi's staff which he cast behind him to stay the demons as they pursued him from the underworld. Offering having been made to this rod, the conversation of the passers-by was earnestly listened to. Another method of later origin required the co-operation of three maidens. Repairing to a place where roads crossed, they thrice repeated an invocation to the deity of ways, marked out a space over which they scattered rice to drive away evil spirits, and then, having drawn their fingers along the teeth of a boxwood[1] comb, stationed themselves, each on a different road, waiting to catch the words of people going by. Dreams, strange to say, do not seem to have been regarded in the light of important supernatural revelations, though auguries were occasionally drawn from them, and the service of interpreting them has, of course, found professors. Sometimes an augury was sought by standing under a bridge and listening to the patter of feet overhead; sometimes the familiar device of pitching coins was employed, and sometimes divine revelations were supposed to be conveyed in the sounds made by a priest whistling by inhalation. It need scarcely be said that the old custom of trial by ordeal, to which allusion is made in previous chapters, has disappeared, but there still exists a device for detecting guilt which, though not disfigured

FENCING.

[1] The Japanese term for boxwood (*tsuge*) means also "to tell." Hence the above custom.

by physical cruelty, partakes of the nature of an ordeal. It is called *sumi-iro*, or the "color of ink." Let us suppose that a theft has occurred in a household. Then each domestic is required to write a certain word with the same brush and the same solution of Indian ink. The writing should take place, if possible, in the presence of the diviner, but that condition is not essential. Conscience is supposed to betray its working in the lines of the ideographs written. There is in this device a practical element that often secures the desired result. It is on record that when the Emperor Inkyo (411-453 A. D.) commanded the ordeal of boiling water as a means of detecting usurpers of noble names, the guilty folks ran away rather than submit to the test. Something of the same kind frequently happens when the *sumi-iro* device is employed: but, under any circumstances, the tracing of an ideograph involves such an effort of muscular directness and undivided attention that the quality of a suspected person's writing may often have much significance.[1]

The reference that we have just made to the ordeal of boiling water brings us to the confines of a wide realm of superstitions based upon *Shinto* belief in the omnipresence of the tutelary spirits and translated into visible phenomena through the agency of hypnotism. The Japanese seem to have discovered, at a very early period, that an abnormal nervous condition can be produced by concentrated attention and abeyance of the will, and like many other peoples to whom a scientific explanation of the fact had not presented itself, they interpreted the strange condition to mean spirit-possession. Prayer and incantation, preceded by purificatory rites and assisted by violent finger-twistings, were the means employed to produce this mesmeric state, and the person reduced to it became a spirit medium, gifted with the power of performing miracles, of uttering predictions and of curing diseases. The range of miracles was limited to three — sprinkling boiling water over the body without feeling the heat; ascending, on bare feet, a ladder of razor-sharp sword-blades, and walking with naked soles over a bed of live coals,[2] all of which are constantly practised by *Shinto* priests and devotees to this day. It must be noted that these performances do not seem to have been degraded by charlatans in any era into mere money-making spectacles. Their object has always been to vivify religious faith. As for the faculty of vaticination supposed to be developed during the sacred trance, its uses are of the simplest character. It might, indeed, be more accurately described as *clairvoyance*, since it discloses events actually happening beyond the range of normal observation rather than events still lying in the lap of the future. For the rest, it does not occupy any prominent place in the usages or thoughts of the nation. The healing power, however, is frequently invoked; for all sickness and disease being attributed

[1] The simplest and perhaps the most senseless method of divination is by the abacus (*soroban*). Its use is confined to cases of illness. To the number of years that the patient has lived are added the numbers of the month and the day of his birth. The sum thus obtained is multiplied by 3 and divided by 9. If the remainder is 3 or a smaller number, recovery is considered certain. If it is a number between 3 and 6, the case is grave, the danger growing as the remainder ascends. Equal division is counted as a remainder of 9, and signifies certain death.

[2] Mr. Percival Lowell, in "Occult Japan," gives lengthy and most picturesque accounts of these and other cognate performances. They are called *Kami-waza*, or deeds of deities.

to the influence of evil spirits, it seems natural and proper that the tutelary deities should be summoned to drive out these demoniacal tormentors. We confine ourselves here to merely sketching in outline the connections that the *Shinto* creed thus undertakes to establish between its disciples and supernatural beings. To fill in the details of the picture would involve long descriptions of rites and incantations which precede and accompany spirit-possession, but are only accessories, having much the same relation to the central phenomenon as the faceted glass held before a subject's eyes in Europe has to the mesmeric state induced by staring at it.

It will be evident from what has been here set down that the Japanese are an emphatically superstitious people. In their every-day life they tread very closely upon the confines of the supernatural world. Whatever estimate of their intellectual development the fact suggests, it is none the less a fact. Possibly, when we recall the history of Occidental morality from the days of the Alexandrian Platonists to the times of Swedenborg and Werner, and the era of American spirit-materializers and astrologers, we may be less disposed to pronounce harsh judgments on the traditional mysticism which has been handed down from generation to generation in the secluded family circle of the Japanese nation.

JAPANESE TYPES.

* 9 7 8 3 7 4 1 1 2 2 6 3 7 *